TIME,
WAIT

UNIVERSITY OF CENTRAL FLORIDA

Contemporary Poetry Series

George Bogin, *In a Surf of Strangers*
Van K. Brock, *The Hard Essential Landscape*
Gerald Duff, *Calling Collect*
Malcolm Glass, *Bone Love*
Susan Hartman, *Dumb Show*
Lola Haskins, *Planting the Children*
Michael McFee, *Plain Air*
David Posner, *The Sandpipers*
Nicholas Rinaldi, *We Have Lost Our Fathers*
Robert Siegel, *In a Pig's Eye*
Edmund Skellings, *Face Value*
Edmund Skellings, *Heart Attacks*

TIME, WAIT

Poems by

Hannah Kahn

A University of Central Florida Book

UNIVERSITY PRESSES OF FLORIDA
Orlando

Library of Congress catalog information appears on the last page of this book.

Skaters' Waltz, © 1975 by *Commonweal*
Cycle, © 1955 by Downe Publishing Co.
Umbilical, © 1968; In the Year of Grace, © 1968; Woodbourne, © 1969;
The Game, © 1969; Chant for the Dead, © 1973; Aboard the *France*, ©
1975; Without Tenure (under the title "The Collector"), © 1975; De-
tours, © 1975; The Limper, © 1975; The Unnamed, © 1975 by Huntsville
Literary Association
Spinster, © 1958 by *The Literary Review*
The Outsider, © 1974 by *Kansas Quarterly*
Notation in Time, © 1970; Without Compass, © 1970 by
Poetry, A Magazine of Verse
Salvation, © 1976 by Southern Methodist University *Southwest Review*
Heritage, © 1951; Ride a Wild Horse, © 1953 (under the title "Into the
Sun") by Saturday Review Associates

Copyright 1983 by the Florida Board of Regents
Printed on acid-free paper in the USA

Acknowledgments

The author is indebted to the following publications in
which certain of these poems first appeared:

*American Scholar, C.C.C.R. Journal, Commonweal, The Courier, Folio, Human Voice Quarterly, Imprints, Kansas
Quarterly, Ladies' Home Journal, Literary Review, Lyric, New
York Times, Poem, Poetry, Saturday Review, Southwest Review, Voices,* and *Weid.*

Grateful acknowledgment is made to Poetry Society of America
for "The Outsider," 1969; to Poetry Society of Georgia for
"Confrontation" (Society Prize, 1969); "Metastasis" (Society
Prize, 1973); "Elegy for Jay" (Society Prize, 1976); to
Jacksonville Council of the Arts for "The Strangeling" 1963; to
Poetry Society of Virginia for "For Sale" (Virginia Commonwealth University Prize, 1976); to Borestone Mountain Poetry Awards: Best Poems of 1964, for "Heritage."

The poem "Haiku" appeared as a preface poem to the
book *Between Parent and Child,* by Dr. Haim Ginott.

"At the Chapel" reprinted by permission from *National Forum:
Phi Kappa Phi Journal,* vol. 63, no. 2 (Spring 1983).

*for all the people I love
and they know who they are
and in loving memory of
Paula Milton, Fred Shaw, and
Suzanne Douglass*

Contents

Ride a Wild Horse

Ride a wild horse
with purple wings
striped yellow and black
except his head
which must be red.

Ride a wild horse
against the sky
hold tight to his wings

before you die
whatever else you leave undone—
once ride a wild horse
into the sun.

1 :: Choosing Tigers

Confrontation

He who chooses tigers makes
A covenant with fear
Trades eiderdown and marigolds
For terror, measures air
Against the momentary thrust,
The crucial undefined
Confrontation in the woods,
The torment in the mind.

He who chooses tigers takes
A pathway marked with blood,
Trades road signs for the unexplored
Jungle where the dead
Inscribed their messages on stone,
Forsook the tender bed.

He who chooses tigers breaks
A crucible of tears
Trades flesh that yields and bone
That finds enclosure for the spears
Of cactus and the thorn that draws
Blood from dormant stone.

Heritage

Someday I shall gather up
All the pieces of myself;
Something of the song that stayed
In my mind when Nero played;
Something that I left in Greece
Could it be that Socrates
Drinking hemlock, knew that I
Would someday be afraid to die
And drank the bitter brew for me
To prove the final victory?

Someday I shall gather up
All the pieces of myself;
Something Sappho tried to say
When she spoke to me one day;
Something Moses said for me,
Chanting, "Set my people free."
Mary crying at the cross
While I shared her grief and loss.
The wall of China holds and stands
Because I built it with my hands.

I was born long years ago
With roots in towns I do not know;
Roots that grow within my mind
With thorns and blossoms intertwined—
I who in another age
Used a tablet for a page
Look up to the sky and know
That I am part of long ago.

Woodbourne

There was Bessie the cow and Henry who fed her
And the house with the turrets that windowed the sky;
The leaded panes of glass where the world
Took on the colors of red and green
And the morning shimmer of blue, but yellow
Was always the color that held me suspended,
Breathless in time for the street washed in light.

There was time that year when I was twelve
To watch the sun melt and dissolve in the sky,
Time to run panting down a mountain,
Gather berries, thrust myself
On the dark earth moist with dampened leaves
When the grass was green and the grass was God.

The sap ran thick from the maple tree
And autumn droned till winter shook
Her white fist at the shivering town
And a swath of crimson stained the snow
And I was never a child again.

Notation in Time

Remember how the mountain called to us;
How thick the huckleberries, purpled-blue
Filled up the pails we carried to the house
And how our hands were stained. With this
Reminder of the past I write to you
With love and memory like worn out shoes
That leave the imprint of the places they
Once trod upon; the holy and profane
Citadels they desecrated. Now I write
Trying to resurrect a long-gone day.

Answer me, friend, before the barren vine
Atrophies and makes us alien, strange.
Guilt is a harsh companion and the mind
Sorting the past reveals the ancient stain.
Before the hungry tigers waken, lunge,
Accept the offering from my withered hand.

Umbilical

This portion that I offer you
Is more than weight can bear.
I take the bread,
Nibble it slowly,
Knowing that your share
Consumed, retains a measure of the seed
The ritual of sustenance by blood.

Sometimes I think your body
Holds the stem
From which all lilies bloom.
I gather you unto myself
As though a surging hymn
Accompanied the rites.
Here you grow
Contained by innocence,
Insurgent, new.

Without Compass

It is as though I lived in time
That rises up in waves
While I attempt to hold the tide
With long white silken gloves.

As though I, deafened by a sound,
Spoke yet could not hear
My own voice nor the warning bell
That stammered in the air.

And Why Is the Tower Burning

The woman who dances in the middle of the room
Is a very old woman before her time

Her shrivelled skin lies at her feet
And she stumbles over the patterned years

> *Sun burn brighter*
> *The woman is cold*
> *Burn fiercer   burn faster*
> *Thaw the frost in her bones*

I will arise from this coffined bed
And dance again with the man who comes
Out of the shadows

> *Dance with me Henry*
> *Dance with me now*

> *London Bridge is falling down*
> *And why is the tower burning*

> *Faster and faster*
> *Whirl me around*
> *Dance with me over*
> *And under the ground*

I will hear the music
I will know the sound
When the walls stop turning
Around in the room
And there is no bridge
From my bed to the tomb

Driving Home

You drive down Northeast Second Avenue
Pass Corre Cleaners
The five-and-dime
Bob and Betty's

You turn right on 36th Street
The cat you almost hit
Turns into the alley

THE BEAST won't be open until 6 o'clock
There's a black leopard painted on the door
It follows you
Even after you leave the place

Someday
You'll take this ride
The car will stop running
The bank won't open
You'll walk back to the house
Turn on the switch
Nothing will happen
And the stranger
Staring at you from the mirror
Will be you

End of Summer

The tree leans downward, beckoning
The hand to pick the ripened fruit.
I, the witness, stand and wait,
Watch a bird invade the sky,
The hour grows late.

Yet in this moment held in time,
The tree, the bird, the fruit are all
Contained within this interval,
This motionless containment of
The essence held by summer's end.

Family History

My name is Eve
My husband is Adam
My address is Eden
And I have two sons

One is Cain
One is Abel—
(My whole life
Sounds like a fable)

There was an apple
And there was a snake
What a mistake
For a woman to make. . . .

We'll have to find
Another town
It might take ages
To live this down.

Eve

After she ate the apple
And knew she had made her bed,
I think that Eve smiled softly
And patted the snake on the head.

Women's Club Luncheon

After the fruit cup
Beautifully served
    (forget the wilted grapes;
    the soggy berries)

They talk about the president
Who made a speech
    (she really shouldn't be praised
    it's they to whom thanks are due)

The number for the door prize
Is now called
    (an indrawn breath—
    her number, once removed)

The fashion show is next
The new fall styles
    (the girl who wears the suit is really slim
    why do the sizes range from four to ten?)

But look into their eyes
Beyond the words
All emptiness exposed
Count time, count lines,
Count loneliness that traps them like a noose
With just enough small space to let them breathe.

Time, Wait

I have to see the Statue of Liberty
And I have to see the Metropolitan Museum of Art

When I was nine years old my class went
But Mickey Berman talked me into going to
A live vaudeville show
Where Navarro was playing or dancing or something

I wanted to go to the Met
But I was so proud that Mickey asked me
To go with her

Anyway it's important now that I get to see the
Statue of Liberty
Everybody has to get someplace at least once
Otherwise it's like a label without an address
Or a passport without a destination

Or like my life
That never knew which way it had to go
So it stood still too long

2 :: Detours

Aboard the *France*

I think of you standing on deck
Leaning on a rail
Fixing your eyes on a point in space
Aware that they in the cabin below
Cross currents

Look in the water
See there the golden boys
Swimming toward you

If only the boat would stop
Or time

The Game

Almost the moment is now
When I speak to her
The sleeve of her flannel robe
Brushes my cheek
And I am child again
And we parry each other's words

"When I am old, will you?"
I laughed and said, "No,
I'll have other things to do";
Now the mood is merged
With separate clouds that converge
And the moon that was blurred
Is suddenly whole again.

She reaches out
I almost touch her hand
While she moves through orbits of memory.
But the future is now her past
And the words belong to a ghost
And I am chilled by the bantering phrase
That moved like a volley ball
Between us two
When I won the game by default

Detours

You have learned them well
The roads a man can take
Where markings show the detours
Yours

DEAD END

Waiting
Having patience
Aware of how his hand
Rested upon his lap

Signs
Like sentinels
That guard the entrance
To unhallowed ground

You do not even face him when you talk
Instead
You speak to me
Make gestures   smile

Only your voice betrays you
And your hand
That taps the frosted glass
And codes his name

Without Tenure

You wrote
      each letter curling inward
      the punctuation
      correct, precise
      as though you placed a seal
      on what you said
      the hallmark of your tense
      constricted style

You walked
      thinking of the blow
      that might be hurled
      no expert at Karate
      you withdrew

You talked
      as though a barrier existed
      which, if hurdled
      would lead into a thicket
      unexplored

You stopped
      your eyes behind the lens
      Reflecting gold
      The miser's hoard
      Acquisitive and haunted
      You vaulted time

A Word to Bridge the Pause

In that small area between
The noun and verb the moment is
Suspended while I forage for
A word to bridge the pause

And in the moment's servile time
Servile yet proud in that it will
Not bend itself nor yet conform
The word defies the interval.

Noun and verb can make complete
The thought without the notes of grace;
And yet I probe into myself
To resurrect a certain place,
A certain mood, a certain time,
Containing grace notes for a rhyme.

The Limper

There is a dry rot in my bones
Of metaphors and old clichés
Syllables in patterned rows
That permeate the thought, the phrase.
The tension yields and I become
Like a juggler tossing nouns,
Adjectives and wilted verbs,
Worn-out, shoddy, hand-me-downs.
There is a dry rot in my bones,
I stub my toes on ancient stones.

Take Words

Splash red on the wall
On the floor
On the page

See it explode
In an outburst
Of rage

See it expand
Dissolve
In a stain

Take red for the terror
The thrust
Of pain

That even in shadows
Leaves halos
That glow

Take words
To counter
The ultimate blow

Note to a Young Poet

Not from the shallow thrust
Of bird defying wind;
Take motion from the hawk's
Convulsive claw

The tension in your mind
Compels the living word;
Deflect the facile phrase,
Temper the blurred.

Strip flesh until the bone
Emerges marrow-filled;
Point arrows to the sun
Direct and disciplined.

Late Evening

The landscape blurs
The trees are leaning down
Their branches move
As though, with folded leaves,
They prayed.

I walk among the leaves
I watch them fall
Each leaf becomes a word,
Each word becomes a poem
I did not write.

The Manuscript Unbound

Now she is gone and all the house is still,
Her desk, her pen, the manuscript unbound
Speak silently for her, reach out until
I take them in my hands. There is no sound
Other than what is echoed by the past.
I read her poems again, I feel them break
Like moments out of time that could not last.

Now she is gone. Perhaps she watches me.
While I am reading, sitting in her chair
All that was hers attains identity,
Her words become alive and fill the air.
I smile because one line has so much charm,
And almost feel her hand upon my arm.

For Sale

The house is empty now. They moved last year
I never spoke to them when they lived here.
The woman seemed harassed, she'd seldom speak
And when she did, the words were never clear.
The children were destructive, they would tear
The flowers from the vine and trample them
And sometimes when the wind was right, I'd hear
Strange sounds, strange voices, almost like a hymn
Pervasive, haunting, then the lights grew dim.

Now they are gone. The grass untrampled, green;
The flowers bloom; the dogs no longer bark;
But something ominous, unnamed, unseen,
Hovers in the air, and when it's dark
I see a flickering light, a glowing spark,
Deep in the attic, then it goes away.
The shadows seem to move, the night grows stark,
Terror closes in. The sky is grey
And I become the guardian and the prey.

Metastasis

The cells divide
And multiply
My body is
Their battleground
I am the field
They occupy

The needle moves
Against my flesh
Patterned sound
Invades the mind
I feel the edge
Of every stitch

Ether dulls
The moving light
Focuses
Intensifies
Shifting tones
Of white on white

I shuffle names
That do not mesh
My fingers bridge
The weighted air
The clock is frozen
To the wall

Sonogram

Immersed in warm water   fearful
Of my own breathing
Having been told to lie quietly
I think of the women
In the waiting room
The wrinkled one
Whose belly is swollen
The one who is so thin
Her dressing gown keeps slipping
Off her shoulders
And the one who keeps asking
For her husband

They said he couldn't come in
The waiting room was too small
And only patients were allowed.
She kept walking to the door
To make sure he was still in the hall

The warm water becomes seductive
Hypnotic
In the water I see their faces
I am looking at them
And suddenly I see

Skeletons   skulls   bones
And I point at them

It is you
It is you
It is you
No, it is . . .

Woman Alone

Squeezing the word till it breaks,
I forge the poem

In the sidewalk, cracks widen
There is no flower bursting through

Lying in a narrow bed
At the Barbizon Hotel for Women
How do you measure fifty years

Walls keep crowding in
The light is off
Shadows take form
    After marriage, children
    For the first time alone
    Counting time, years
    Exploring cavities

There is no freedom ride
No definition of space

I walk to the door
At the end of the passage
There is another door
Marked EXIT
I turn the knob
Knowing the door will not open

In the Year of Grace

As though a bomb would never fall,
As though one never fell,
I go to shop on Friday night,
My children learn to spell.

As though a word, as though a thought
Has meaning in an age
When bombs explode much louder than
The words on printed page

I take the words and give to them
A portion of the breath
By which a woman, routine-bound
Snaps her thumb at death.

3 :: Betrayal

Awakening

Suddenly
A planet broke
The whole world crashed
And then awoke

And we were two
And we were one
Who saw the turning
Of the sun

We were one
Who saw the skies
Open
To our startled eyes

Aware of a world
Exposed and new
I was myself
And I was you

And all the fragments
Fell in place
I reached my hand
To touch your face

And you were cold
And I grew old

Spinster

The room is quiet.   I alone
Cry myself in me,
Shrouded in the vivid cloak
Of necessity.

Within this darkened room the flesh,
Once rigid, now defiled,
Seeks cloister in the depths of sleep,
Sobs penance like a child.

Six White Horses

What did I want for a nickel and a penny,
Six white horses,
Seven white doves,
Fenced securely
In possession,
What can you buy for a small-change love?

What can you buy for a nickel and a penny?
Crashing thunder?
Falling stars?

Enough to know that somewhere
Six white horses
Break the fences
Race the wind—

And the white doves,
Even wounded,
Once knew rapture, blinding light,
Once knew clouds as a blanket

When they fell
They fell from height

The Ledge

We sleep together and we share
The ritual of a marriage bed;
There is no child as testament,
Nothing to seal the chasm where
There is no flowering of seed.

We cling with desperation to
A ledge that is precarious;
Knowing that one word could undo
The tenuous rope that binds us now
And yet by force could strangle us.

We sleep together and we know
The alienation that compels
The bitter word. With grace we go
Each to our separate crucible
And watch the night corrode the sky.

A Cat Called Kat

I fear your lunge, you fear my thrust,
This truce of ours is nebulous,
Yet neither understates what must
Be perilous for both of us.

I bristle at your cool disdain
You spit with venom at my fist
Yet I am ravished by your pain;
Your paw soothes my trembling wrist.

Christmas Eve, 1972

It was good soup
Thick with the barley that swelled
Marrow bones
Chunks of beef
Potatoes and carrots cut thick
Slivers of garlic

Outside the angry wind
Threatened the trees
Here, with the firelight tinting the walls
We sit
Frank and the child and I

I think of the homeless
After the quake
Of the old men
Laying out coins

There are things in this passing year
I do not want to recall
Memories forcing their way
Into my being

But God, let me give thanks
That tonight, in this one place,
This one time,
Three who need each other,
Break bread, eat soup.

Room 732

I tell you how much better it will be
After it's over. And you, with tubes of plasma,
Needle-pricked, lower your eyelids
Try to force a smile.
The anonymous intern passes by the door.

Outside the windows I can see the cars
Flashing their signal lights as they make the turn
Until all cars converge in one thin line,
Following arrows,
Guiding them toward home.

For you, your home is here, your destiny
Held by the drops of plasma.
You start to speak but the words
Are blurred by a cough.

What can I say to you—
Talk of the way the children help in the house . . .
We hear the crash
Later the siren's screech
Reechoes in this room.
The roses by your bed
Are deadly still.

One Year Later

I have no words with which to spell the night.
I walk into our room, your bed is made,
Your clothes all neatly hung (they always were),
The brass bell on the table left for you
To call me (which you never used)
You proud in all the ways a man can be
Whose bones were molded intricately fine,
And now your bones are crumbling in your grave,
And I must salvage what I could not save.

How shall I bridge the days now you are gone,
Rereading letters, filing things away,
Shuffling the words that throb, the empty night,
And yet there are no tears, the voice is still,
The agony is dormant and I sleep
The troubled sleep of one enmeshed in guilt
Who heard you calling in the tortured night
And did not hear the bell you never rang.

Betrayal

We are diminished by our innocence.
Deranged by platitudes we stand inert,
Embalmed in life.   The fluid drained,
The bone crumbles.   It's late—

I walk among the headstones in my sleep—
I read the names, the dates. I place two stones
Upon your grave. I ask you to forgive
That in some strange, distorted way I live.

4 :: Rhythmed in Silence

Haiku

Child, give me your hand
That I may walk in the light
Of your faith in me

The Outsider

The children move in clusters
Two and three;
The dark-haired one
Stands by the fence
Pulls at her dress
Stares at her shoes
Her shadow
Now grotesque
Is like an image
Mimicking herself.

A pebble on the ground
Is in her way
She steps on it
With such intensity
The force could pulverize
The stone
Had she the strength.

The bell has rung
The children all go in;
She lingers for a little while
Then lagging
Dragging
Follows
While her eyes
Search for a sign
Invisible
Unseen.

The Strangelings

They always have such lovely names;
Melissa, Isla, Valerie, Dale:
As though in naming them there was
A premonition of their bleak
Commitment and the barren days.

The world in which they live is small;
Controlled, constricted, limited,
With fences they may never climb,
Doors that are too often locked,
Language they may never learn,
And yet their names reflect the sun.

Cycle

Now is the cycle broken. Now the moon
Who was the mother to the turning tide
Has left me rudderless, remote, alone,
With this dull ache diminishing my pride
In being woman, being one who has
Within herself the movement of the earth,
And now forsaken, drained. The years that pass
Take more than shoreline, more than cancelled birth.

I whose body knew the rhythmic flow,
Who was attuned to change that did not change
But followed in a pattern I could know
Am now bewildered by this sudden strange
Distortion of the music stirring me
Who never was attuned to quiet sea.

My daughter walks in light. I watch her walk.
She has not passed this threshold lost to me
Nor is she yet aware that shadows stalk
To intercept a child who will not be
For long a child. The static moon will turn,
The waters ripple and the waves will rise;
She will not be prepared, yet she will learn,
She who will be by instinct woman-wise.

Tonight the moon is full and by its light
My daughter walks. The world grows inward, small,
Drawing us closer in this quiet night,
Making more meaningful this interval . . .
This threshold that I leave where she will soon
Be as was I, a daughter to the moon.

Skater's Waltz

I remember my aunt
(God rest her soul)
How she called the children
Into the room
And commanded our silence
While Betty played
"The Skater's Waltz."

It wasn't the song
Nor Betty playing;
It was my aunt
Who stood by the piano
And turned the pages,
That I remember.

I was a child
In that long-ago time
But whenever I hear
A young child play
I think of my aunt,
Regal and proud,
Who turned the pages
And made us listen.

Convalescent Home

In the far corner
Almost obscured by the shadows
A woman slowly rocks
In a chair that is not a rocker
And hums, over and over,
A song she learned as a child

As though that was all she remembered
As though the faded years
Blurred in the fog-like mist
That led to the desolate passage

From which there is no escape
From which there is no returning
Only the plaintive song
Repeated in the twilight

At the Chapel

The man who lived in the apartment above his
said he was a real nice man

Barbara told me she owed him $10. and what
did I want her to do with it.

Then the man from the funeral parlor
motioned to me
and called me into the private office
      wood-paneled, linen-draped,
      clean ash tray, new book of matches
      pens ready for the signatures

      this air-conditioned office
      where all conditions are met and aired

I signed all the papers
I nodded my head

I'll go home and this Sunday
he won't call me to see
if I've made it through the week

Tomorrow
after the funeral
I'll decide where the flowers should go

Homecoming

I see him now
His eyes lock into mine
Across the space where words
Cannot be heard

I want to run
To hold him but I wait

He comes toward me
I resurrect his face
It is not his

This time away has made
This stranger
Marked

He comes toward me
I look for words
To bridge the months

We stand together now
Transfixed
Nailed to the ground
That does not yield.

I take his work-worn hand
Into my own
He fumbles with his coat

We walk toward home
The light has changed
Where brightness limned the leaves
The shadows place a pall

Soon night will shield
His eyes from mine

Kaddish

(for Marilyn)

As long
As I speak
Your name
You are
Not dead

As long
As I think your pain
I cannot
Grieve

The granite marker
Tells
Your name
Your age

The bleak horizon
Scars
The barren hedge

As long as I
You
Are not dead.

5 :: Past the Rock

Chant for the Dead

I walk along the shoreline
Picking up
Shells that are broken
Bottle caps
The bathers left last summer

The waters rise
The ocean beats against
The rock on which I stand.
Father, I cry,
Speak now.
I try to clutch your robe.
The cloth dissolves.

Your silence seals the day.

That a Man Can Tell

I will make a poem out of plain words
That a child could know
That a woman could feel
That a man could say over and over again

I will say what I believe
Knowing truth is a variable

I will say what I feel
Knowing feelings cannot be said

I will say they endured though they died
I will speak of pity and love
That were not heard

I will say how the silent men stood by

I cannot say it all
I will try.

Elegy for Jay

Mourn for this child the days he spent alone;
The way he stared with eyes remote and glazed
And never reached the toy he reached out for.
Mourn for this child that he could never say
The words that needed saying, nor could he
In any way discern the intervals
That would determine when she would appear.

Within this sterile ward where beds have rails
And needles etch their signatures of pain
He waited to be lifted, to be fed,
For blurs of white to intercept the space
That kept receding further from his sight.
Mourn for this child that on his days on earth
His boundaries were cast.

Two Steps, Three Steps, Four . . .

Two black steps and a purple wreath
A small child crawls unaware that death
Is a marble rolling toward a slab of sleep
And a curled leaf withering on a wind-tossed heap.

Three black steps and a yellow spool
Where the thread unwinds in a spiral coil—

Four more steps and the light comes through
Where the steps point down and the road for you
Is no road at all but a steep incline
Where you stand or jump from a thin taut line.

Salvation

He was dressed like the man from the Rescue Mission
Holding a copper plate
Asking for money

In the dream I had nothing to give him
I tore at my pockets, my clothes, my purse,
As though something, a coin, a bill,
Something,
It was as though
If I couldn't find it
There would never be salvation for anyone
Everything depended on me
And I had no coins

Then I started beating on the man
Not being able to stop the blows, the thrusts,
While he shielded his face with his hands,
While he kept backing into the corner

Outside I heard a siren
The day was a red scream

Past the Rock

How far do I have to dig
To get past the rock

Everything fights back
I put the shovel aside
And stare at the sullen ground

My fingers turn blue
My body swells
At night I strip fat
And emerge
Like a stalk stripped of leaves
No longer insulated
I stand exposed.

The Jungle

I keep them muzzled stealthily
The wolves that howl and threaten me
Yet they remain, a portent of
A force that struggles, lacking love
Their violent lunge stays my breath,
Foretells a time of sudden death.

Implicit in this fear I curl
Inward. How am I to hurl
The demons out, the quivering flesh
Is moist and clammy to my touch.

And I am vulnerable. There is
No one to hear the throttled voice,
The struggle is the wolves' and mine,
Their howling turns into a whine . . .
And then I fall asleep, no drums
Will beat until tomorrow comes.

Weeds

Tonight, when the town is asleep
I shall gather weeds

I shall tie them together
And pile them into a mound
And they shall arise
Like a monument out of the ground

Tonight I shall gather weeds
That I did not plant

This be my harvest of struggle
This interval
Of weeds untended
Yet strangely durable

The Unnamed

When in the utltimate darkness
I rest
Who never knew rest in the bright
Glare of the sun
Who never once was warmed
Except from need

When, as I said before, and must say again,
In the darkness I have not known
Yet felt within
As black
(though black holds part of light)

When I disavow
All color   all tone
All semblance to lustre,
Sleep naked, unshrouded, unkempt
In the ultimate dark

Be to me answering voice
Fulfill in me
The unnamed   unspoken   unknown

Make litany
Of the words I dared not say
Speak them for me

Diary Note

This is the way I lean my head
Against the shoulder
Of the dead

They knew the harsh insistence of
A patterned world
Deflecting love

The scurrying for post and place
The slurred and smothered
Words of grace

So for today
I lean my head
Shield my body
Break my bread

Hannah Kahn, of Miami, Florida, is a well-published
author, teacher, poet-in-residence, and workshop and conference
leader. From 1958 to 1974, she was poetry editor of
the *Miami Herald*.

Mrs. Kahn's awards include the International Sonnet Competi-
tion of the Poetry Society of Great Britain and Amer-
ica, the Westminster Award, the Jane Judge Award, the
Jacksonville Council of Arts Award, the Virginia
Commonwealth University Award, the Conrad Aiken Award,
and an annual award of the Poetry Society of America.

In 1962 she published a volume of poetry called *Eve's Daugh-
ter*, which is in its fifth edition. Her work has been
included in textbooks and anthologies in the United States,
Canada, Great Britain, and Australia, and her poems
have been published by such diverse periodicals as *American
Scholar, Harpers Magazine, Southwest Review,
Prairie Schooner, New York Times, Ladies' Home Journal, Sat-
urday Review, American Mercury, Commonweal, Poetry,
Christian Science Monitor, and National Forum.*

University Presses of Florida, the agency of the State
of Florida's university system for publication of scholarly and
creative works, operates under policies adopted by
the Board of Regents. Its offices are located at 15 Northwest
15th Street, Gainesville, Florida 32603.

Library of Congress Cataloging in Publication Data
Kahn, Hannah
    Time, Wait

    (University of Central Florida contemporary poetry
series)
    I. Title.   II. Series.
    PS3561.A365T5   1983   811'.54   83-12565
    ISBN 0-8130-0775-5